Press Release Distribution, Media Monitoring, Communication and Graphics services – Look No Further

The All-in-One Shop for Media and Communication Services

Send your Press Releases for Less and Get a Free Language Edition.

>> Increase your competitiveness with our packages

>> Be the news in every language

>> We take your news to local and global news media

>> Media contact and press release services

Media Monitoring, Analysis, and Measurement Services

>> TV and Radio News Monitoring

>> Online News and Social Media Monitoring

>> Monitor Competition

>> Measure PR & Marketing Effectiveness

>> Automate Daily, Weekly & Monthly Reports

Graphics and Communication Collateral Services

>> Print: Newsletters, Postcards, Calendar Design, Layout

>> Social Media: Campaign Management, Design

>> Website Design, Graphics

>> Video: Shooting, Producing, Editing

>> Advert/Media Buying Services

>> Printing Quotes

Start Today @ www.globalprplus.com
or Call: 1-832 857 2572

Editor's Comment

Special Report- An International Media Tour of the Manufacturing, Oil and Gas Facilities in CORE PA

USA Oil and Gas Monitor representing the United States Energy publication for the oil and gas industry and other international journalist from the United Kingdom, Australia, India and Nigeria; at the request of CORE PA Global-tour some of Pennsylvania's innovative companies and industrial suppliers involved in the mining, oil and gas field machinery manufacturing industries.

The purpose- CORE PA Global is an initiative established to increase the visibility of a 53-county footprint of Pennsylvania, to international and domestic investors. CORE PA partners with over 50 economic development organizations and the Commonwealth of Pennsylvania to attract, retain, and grow business and industry in the region.

Putting it simple- Noelle A. Long Project Manager & Regional Representative CORE PA Global said, "We are tasked with telling the story of the rest of Pennsylvania because often times, people just associate Pittsburgh and Philadelphia as the whole state, but there is more of a story to tell to promote the more rural regions of the state. We are doing this through promotion like the media familiarization tour we are doing right now".

Hence, this edition report its findings during the tour.

Our Event- The international pipeline, oil and gas safety conference March 14-16, 2017, POGS '17- Early Registration Open and Call for Abstract still on going. Register Today @ http://oilandgassafetyconference.com

Happy Independence and happy Reading.

Gloria Towolawi- Editor

Editor-in-Chief
Gloria Towolawi

Europe Bureau
Esther Coker

Nigeria Bureau
David Arhavbarien

Contributing Editor
Gloria Instead

Reporter
Caleb Motinwo

Advert & Marketing
Jewel Spring
T: 832-486-0095
E: advertise@usaoilandgasmonitor.com

Distribution & sales
Richard Godfirst

Subscribers Service
E: subscribe@usaoilandgasmonitor.com

RGT Media Communications Corp.
Publishers of
USA Oil and Gas Monitor
Workplace Weekly News
GlobalPRPlus

USA Oil and Gas Monitor is published 12 times a year monthly by RGT Media Communications Corp. 10777 Westheimer #1100

Houston, Texas 77042
Subscription price is $144 per year.
Digital copy $9.99 per download.

Copyright 2016 by
RGT Media Communications Corp.

All rights reserved. No part of this publication may be reproduced without the express permission in writing by the publisher or the original author.

Contents

Chilean Mine Rescue puts Center Rock Drilling Technology on Global Spotlight 4

CORE PA – Provides a Distinct Advantage and an Ideal Location for Energy Intensive Industries 7

JWF the Largest Manufacturing Plant in the East serves the Oil and Gas Industry among Other Industries in CORE PA 11

Curry Supply Products support both Drilling and Fracking Operations in the Oil and Gas Industry 13

Photos from Media Tour 16

CORE PA poised to Attract International Trade and FDI to the Oil and Gas, Mining Industries in rural Pennsylvania 18

Ezeflow Group the Largest Manufacturer of Pipe Fitting in North America 22

Shell Cracker Plant Coming to Pennsylvania- Stakeholders and Communities React 23

CAB World Class Cable Rings and Saddles manufactured by the blind and handicap in CORE PA 25

Oring Sunnyside Energy Park Project shows CNG/LNG as a Viable Alternative Fuel 28

Noise Solutions Incorporated provide Turnkey Solutions for the Energy and Mining Industries 31

From left- David Pietrzykowski, President and CEO Center Rock and Brandon Fisher Center Rock Founder

Chilean Mine Rescue puts Center Rock Drilling Technology on Global Spotlight

On the media tour of the oil and gas, mining industries in CORE PA- our first bus stop was Center Rock Inc. CRI whose brand became recognized for its role in the historic Chilean Mine Rescue incident – which was successfully carried out through the intervention of Center Rock – a drilling technology company located in rural Pennsylvania- in CORE PA region of Berlin.

The historic event which took place on August 22, 2010, in which the world was shocked to find out that 33 men trapped in a San Jose, Chile mine were alive in a safe room – 17 days after the mine collapsed.

Brandon Fisher, then President and CEO of Center Rock, Inc. CRI in Berlin, PA knew his company had the tools and technology to rescue the miners before the projected Christmas date. After almost two weeks of providing information and validity to the Center Rock Plan, Brandon and his team flew to the rescue site and provided hands-on assistance. In what would later become to be known as "Plan B", CRI used their Down-the-Hole DTH drilling technology to open the initial 5.5" hole to 12". The next step was to use CRI's Low Profile LP Drill, which eventually broke through on October 9, 2010, 33 days after drilling began. Brandon and his Center Rock team worked around the clock and ultimately played a key role in this historical rescue mission. This team's "Never Say Quit" attitude and their innovative ideas and technology impacted the lives of 33 men and their families. Over the next few days, the 33 miners were rescued from 2043 feet 622.7m below the surface and the last man was hoisted out of the shaft in the Fenix rescue capsule on October 13, 2010.

USAOGM Editor, Gloria Towolawi in a one on one interview with the current President of Center Rock Inc. David Pietrzykowski has this to say about his company products and technology.

USAOGM-Tell about yourself and what you do at Center Rock?

CRI-My name is David Pietrzykowski and I was born and raised in Massachusetts. I attended the University of Oklahoma where I received my BS in Petroleum Engineering. I worked for Ingersoll-Rand for 15 years and most recently Atlas Copco for 10 years. I joined Center Rock as President and CEO in April of 2015.

USAOGM- Give us a brief history of Center Rock and Your products line?

CRI- Center Rock designs and manufactures a complete line of percussive rock drilling tools. The company was founded in 1998 as a service company for oil and gas contractors as well as providing products and services to the domestic US foundation drilling customer base. Aside from standard mono-

hammers and bits from 3.5" to 36" in diameter, Center Rock also produces LP canister drills from as small as 12" for HDD work to the largest ever built 132" LP hole opener. Center Rock is the "proven world leader in canister drill technology". Other specialty products include; ROTO LOC casing advancement systems, Hydro Jaw breakout units, Wassara water hammers, and other specialty products for underbalanced drilling in the Oil and Gas patch.

USAOGM Editor, Gloria Towolawi in a one on one interview with the current President of Center Rock Inc. David Pietrzykowski

USAOGM- What make your Products different from the competition?

CRI- Center Rock prides itself in delivering tailored drilling solutions to its worldwide customer base. In addition, we have a staff of sales individuals who are recognized as some of the most experienced consultants when it comes to drilling holes in rock and overburden. Lastly, we have the technical support to ensure that our products are applied properly and are safely drilling at the highest level of productivity.

USAOGM- Given the historic Chilean mine rescue of August 2010, in which your company helped to accomplish with your drill technology, how has this helped to positions the services you offer as well as your products.

CRI- Center Rock was not globally known prior to the rescue, as the company was focused on a few finite niche markets. The Chilean mine rescue thrust the company into the global spotlight and ensured a more recognizable brand.

USAOGM- Pennsylvania is the second largest natural gas producer in the USA, what role does your products plays in the oil and gas industry.

CRI- Center Rock has from Day one focused on the Marcellus and Utica plays in Ohio, West Virginia, and Pennsylvania. We sell and rent tools directly to the drilling companies that work in the Tristate area. At this time, we are expanding our reach to gain a foothold in the global underbalanced drilling market segment. We provide the hammers and bits that they would use for underbalanced drilling and gas drilling.

Advanced engineering of Center Rock's Low Profile Canister Drills provide a cost effective solution for drilling excavation requirements up to 144" 3658 mm in diameter. Our drills have been used by some of the nation's largest building, roadway, utility and mining contractors to quickly drill holes to the exact size required by their specifications.

Center Rock- Manufacturer of the largest Low Profile Canister Drills in the World

CRI - we are able to extrapolate the Low Profile Canister Drills to any size that the market demand. What we are building currently is a two full-face LP's, a 72 inch and an 84 inch. We are building two hole openers which will have a nose on them, that is 84 inch. Then the outside will be 108 inches in diameter and then you will go one more size to 132 inches in diameter. Two hole openers and two full-faced canister

Center Rock low profile canisters drills current order being built

USA Oil and Gas Monitor
For Daily News Report and Analysis • www.usaoilandgasmonitor.com

International media tour to Center Rock

drills is the order going through right now. That is an 11 foot diameter rock socket and it is massive!

As far as we know, that is the biggest that is ever been produced, so we are excited about it; extrapolating this product to meet a lot of different market requirements.

The low profile canisters drills themselves are quite unique. There is a couple of competitors out there that have tried to make these tools, but the population of tools that we have in the world, no one comes close. Really, what makes our tool unique is, we have gone through the learning curve. We have been building these now for almost 20 years, so over that time we have refined the design to the point where we get the appropriate longevity out of the component, and the performance that the customer's looking for.

It comes down to tailoring solutions for our customers. We do not build products and put them on the shelf and expect everyone to just use what is available. We like to find out. What is the job? What are the parameters of the job? What is the unique environment that you are in and the challenges and obstacles that you are facing? Then we look to design something specifically for the customer. **That ability to be nimble and move on a design, on an immediate basis, gets us the type of flexibility that most big companies do not have. They will still be in meetings, for weeks, we will already be done building it.**

For us, what we are concentrating on is taking this technology and spreading it into other niche markets.

Like we mentioned before, primarily this had been used in construction. Now we are using this in mining; horizontal directional drilling, and to drill utility pole holes. We are taking that technology and extrapolating it into many different market segments.

USAOGM Editor, Gloria Towolawi inside the Fenix rescue capsule

USA Oil and Gas Monitor
For Daily News Report and Analysis • www.usaoilandgasmonitor.com

Paul A. McCloskey, VP of Energy and Business Development Clearfield County

CORE PA – Provides a Distinct Advantage and an Ideal Location for Energy Intensive Industries

Paul A. McCloskey, VP of Energy and Business Development Clearfield County in Core PA makes the case why Energy Intensive Industries should relocate to CORE PA in an interview with Gloria Towolawi – USAOGM.

USAOGM - Tell us about yourself, and what you do?

CAD - I am Paul A. McCloskey. I hold a business degree from Penn State University and began my career in economic development when I was hired as "VP of Energy" with the Clearfield County Economic Development Corporation CCEDC in 2011. At that time, I was focused on assisting companies in the upstream sector of the oil & gas industry that were involved in the development of the Marcellus Shale. A lot of my time was spent developing relationships with the exploration & production companies that were leasing properties & exploring for natural gas in Clearfield County, Pennsylvania. I was charged with being a local liaison for these companies to learn about and be responsive to their needs in our community. I was very involved with helping E&P companies educate the local business & political leaders, as well as the general public, about the unconventional drilling process.

In addition to assisting the E&P companies, I also worked with oil & gas service companies that were moving into the area. I provided them with assistance to meet their real-estate, logistics, & workforce needs as well as introduce them to partners in the local business community. As the price of natural gas began to decline and companies weren't drilling as actively, I began to focus on outreach & attraction to downstream energy-intense companies that would find our low-cost energy environment advantageous.

In 2013, I was promoted to VP of Energy & Business Development and took over management of a local business financing program along with increasing Clearly Ahead's efforts to attract foreign direct investment. I'm reaching out to all types of industries interested in Clearfield County as a location for their business but with a focus on energy-intense industries.

USAOGM- Give us a brief history of clearly Ahead development- you objectives and goals?

CAD- The Clearfield County Economic Development Corporation CCEDC is a private, non-profit 501(c)(6) corporation that was incorporated in 1999. The mission of the organization is to "Proudly Serve the Community to Create Growth and Opportunity in Clearfield County, Pennsylvania." Due to the confusion of many different entities using the acronym "CCEDC", the organization was rebranded and began operating as "Clearly Ahead Development" in 2015.

Our objectives include business retention, business expansion, and increasing the economic base for Clearfield County, Pennsylvania. We accomplish those objectives through offering economic development services relating to:

- land & building identification & procurement
- business financing programs which include grants, loans, & tax-exempt bonds
- workforce identification & training
- infrastructure development
- brownfield redevelopment

USAOGM- Why do you think that CORE PA is an ideal location for energy intensive industries?

CAD- Energy intensive industries use energy either as a source of power or as an input in their manufacturing process; and sometimes both. With regard to the inputs for any type of manufacturing operation, two things come to my mind; price and supply. If a company is going to use "input A" in their process, they will want to make sure that the price of "input A" is affordable & relatively stable wherever they decide to locate. Additionally, they will want to make sure that wherever they locate has an adequate supply of "input A" since a lack of supply will cause an increase in the price of it. Let's talk about both the price and supply of energy in CORE PA and why it is an ideal location for energy intensive industries.

The United States Energy Information Administration's reserve data, which estimates the total amount of technically recoverable natural gas contained in U.S. shale plays continues to steadily increase and by 2018, the United States is projected to be a net exporter of natural gas. This is very significant because when you produce more of something than you consume, it generally leads to lower prices and less price fluctuation which are both good things from the consumer's standpoint. To understand how much of a game-changer this is for the United States, we have to go all the way back to the 1950's to find the last time that the U.S. was a net natural gas exporter. Since the 1950's, we've historically used more natural gas then we've produced and it was only just a few years ago, that LNG terminals were being constructed on our shores for importation and now those terminals are being reconfigured to become LNG export terminals.

So the United States as a whole is producing more natural gas than ever before and shale plays across the country are the reason for that increase in production. Out of those shale plays, one in particular has been the driving force behind the growth in production and CORE PA is strategically situated on top it; the Marcellus Shale. The Marcellus is the 2nd largest natural gas field in the world with an estimated amount of 141 trillion cubic feet of technically recoverable gas. In addition to the estimates, oil and gas companies are constantly employing best practices & increasing efficiencies so the amount of gas they are able to extract continues to increase. All of these factors combined ensure that CORE PA will have a sufficient supply of affordable natural gas for decades to come. And we haven't even mentioned the Utica Shale or the formations above & below the Marcellus which will provide additional sources of energy! Suffice it to say that CORE PA certainly has an abundant supply of energy which is vital for an energy-intensive manufacturing operation.

So we have discussed supply but what about price? Natural gas is more difficult and expensive to transport than a liquid, such as oil, since it has to be compressed and transported to market through a network of pipelines. That reality has resulted in natural gas being more of a regional commodity and sold at various "hubs" across the country where multiple pipelines intersect. The most familiar hub is the "Henry Hub" in Louisiana and the price for natural gas there sets the benchmark for all other trading hubs across the U.S. The "Henry Hub" price is also what the NYMEX is based on so particular attention is given to that hub by companies & markets across the world. As of June 16, 2016, natural gas was selling for $2.59/MMBtu at the Henry Hub.

CORE PA is home to the "Leidy Hub" which is a natural gas trading hub and local price point for companies buying and selling gas produced in the Marcellus region. Tremendous natural gas production from Marcellus wells combined with a lack of pipeline infrastructure to get the gas out of the region has resulted in natural gas produced in CORE PA currently trading well below the Henry Hub price point. As of June 16, 2016, natural gas was selling for $1.46/MMBtu at the Leidy Hub; which is a discount of $1.13 per unit below Henry Hub. Obviously this is a huge advantage for any company that uses natural gas but particularly for an energy intensive company such as a fertilizer company or power plant that would use millions of units of natural gas per year. Now of course, the price changes daily and the Leidy Hub's advantage is not always going be that pronounced but I can tell that over the past two years, natural gas at the Leidy Hub in CORE PA has averaged about $0.60 below the price at the Henry Hub so it is certainly a significant advantage to an energy-intensive company.

I would like to make one last comment relating to the anticipated longevity of the low-cost energy environment in the United States. Many of the foreign companies I speak with are concerned about how long natural gas prices will remain low in the U.S. Of course, no one can predict the future with 100 per cent certainty, but I can point you to the U.S. Energy Information Administration's Annual Energy Outlook report from 2015. In that report, they forecasted average gas prices at the Henry Hub in 2015 at $3.73/MMBtu, in 2020 at $4.88/MMBtu, and in 2040 at $7.85/MMBtu. With gas at the Leidy Hub almost certain to be selling at or below Henry Hub prices, you can see how CORE PA is positioned to have low-cost energy for decades. Lastly, from the work with E and P companies earlier in my career, I've also established relationships with companies that would entertain natural gas supply contracts either on a fixed price basis, tied to some type of index, or even a tolling arrangement. All of these options can be explored further to give an energy-intensive company a certain level of comfort and security about the future.

USAOGM- What is unique about the CORE PA location?

CAD -Besides the fact that CORE PA is located on top of the 2nd largest natural gas field, being the "Keystone

Pipeline Infrastructure in Clearfield County, PA

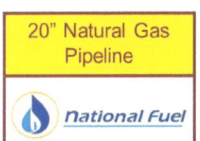
20" Natural Gas Pipeline — National Fuel

30" Natural Gas Pipeline — Dominion

8" LPG Pipeline — TEPPCO

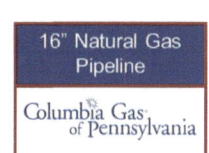
16" Natural Gas Pipeline — Columbia Gas of Pennsylvania

Source: Clearfield County GIS Department (www.gis.clearfieldco.org/)

 "Proudly Serving the Community to Create Growth & Opportunity in Clearfield County, Pennsylvania"

Clearfield County Pipeline Infrastructure

State", we are also strategically positioned in the US and able to service many of the major markets on the east coast including New York, Philadelphia, Baltimore, & Washington D.C., to name a few, within one day's drive. Interstate-80 is the major east-west corridor connecting New York & San Francisco running right through the heart of CORE PA.

Besides our energy resources & strategic positioning, I think what sets CORE PA apart is the work ethic of our citizens. From timber harvesting, to coal mining, and natural gas development, natural resource extraction has been at the core of our local economy for generations and the work ethic that goes along with the nature of those industries has been passed along as well. The first oil well was drilled in the CORE PA region in 1859!

USAOGM- What is the price of natural gas in CORE PA against other locations in the USA e.g. Texas, that can influence companies' decision to re-locate?

CAD - I mentioned above that the current Henry Hub price in Louisiana is $2.59/MMBtu and Leidy Hub price in CORE PA is $1.46/MMBtu. Some other hubs in the U.S. include:

- Agua Dulce Hub - South Texas - $2.25/MMBtu
- Carthage Hub - East Texas - $2.64/MMBtu
- El Paso Permian Hub - West Texas - $2.61/MMBtu
- Chicago NIPSCO Hub - Midwest - $2.70/MMBtu
- CIG Hub - Rocky Mountains - $2.59/MMBtu
- California Regional Avg. - California - $2.88/MMBtu
- Empress Hub - Canada - $2.25/MMBtu

USAOGM - Price is key- but there are other factors that companies will consider before relocating- What infrastructures are in place to influence companies to re-locate here?

CAD - Certainly! Price is key but another major factor relating to natural gas in particular is actually being able to access it. In other words, you have to locate near a pipeline and/or construct a pipeline to your facility in order to take advantage of it. Additionally, the types of energy-intensive industries we are targeting are going to use volumes of gas that are going to necessitate a large diameter pipeline which tends to cost $1 million per mile, or more, to construct. In anticipation of attracting large-volume users, we've worked with our GIS department and mapped out the locations of the existing major transmission pipelines in Clearfield County that can source natural gas from the Leidy Hub. We currently have 3 gas transmission lines ranging in size from 16" to 30" and an 8" LPG pipeline also in the county.

More than likely, if a company is utilizing a large amount of natural gas, they will also need a large amount of electricity and Clearfield County is fortunate to have a 600MW power plant also located in our county. The web of transmission powerlines that emanate from that plant crisscross through the region and we've identified multiple locations where major natural gas pipelines and electricity powerlines intersect. These intersections would be ideal locations for an energy-intensive company to consider locating since it would reduce both the cost & timeline for a company to access those major utilities.

Other existing infrastructure in the region includes excellent railroad infrastructure from the timber & coal mining era. Many of the railroads tended to follow local waterways which provide excellent access to water resources as well.

Access to international airports, ports, & of course traditional interstate routes are all readily available throughout the CORE PA region.

USAOGM - Who are the major players in energy intensive industry in this region?

USA Oil and Gas Monitor

For Daily News Report and Analysis • www.usaoilandgasmonitor.com

CAD - Let me begin answering this by identifying the 7 energy-intensive industries that we feel would enjoy a distinct advantage here: Power Generation, Gas-to-Liquids, Pulp & Paper, Fertilizer, Cement & Brick, Chemicals, and Food & Beverage Processing.

We feel that not only are those industries energy intensive, but we also possess other inputs/advantages in this region that would be attractive to companies in those industries. For instance, CORE PA is a leading source of hardwood timber which provides spin-off opportunities for the Pulp & Paper industry to take advantage of. Commerce Park in Clearfield, PA is the first industrial park to be certified by a 3rd party for food & beverage processing in Pennsylvania. CORE PA used to have a robust brick manufacturing industry due to our access to various shales & clay used in brick manufacturing, etc.

The power generation industry has been the first industry that I'm aware of to really embrace our natural gas resources in order to replace the aging plants that utilized coal for power generation for decades. In that sector, you have NRG Energy, Panda Power Funds, Moxie Energy, and EmberClear that have all announced power generation projects utilizing Marcellus gas that I am aware of.

IMG Midstream is a company that is taking advantage of the low-cost natural gas to launch distributed generation facilities or in other words "mini-power plants". Compass Natural Gas is currently developing the "virtual pipeline" concept whereby they will deliver natural gas to your facility via CNG tanker trunks if you do not have access to a physical pipeline. Lastly, at their manufacturing facility in Wyoming County, PA, Proctor & Gamble decided to drill Marcellus wells on the 1,400 acres that their plant is located on and now they are energy-independent and operating 100 per cent off the grid! And of course, you are aware of the Shell cracker plant in Beaver County, PA.

As far as the major players in those other industries, I am currently working with some companies but they are confidential at this point.

USAOGM - Tell us about shell cracker plant coming to CORE PA and how this will benefit the economic well-being of the community and businesses?

CAD - I am excited about what it means for the rest of Pennsylvania's economy! The Shell cracker plant will be located in Beaver County, PA which is actually just outside of the CORE PA region. Regardless though, it's a fantastic announcement and this decision will essentially create an entirely new industry in western-PA.

USAOGM - How does the location of cracker plant by Royal Dutch shell helps build your case?

CAD - Well, I think it helps to vindicate all of the reserve estimates and production potential that many of the geologists have been suggesting since Shell certainly believes that there will be sufficient ethane available at affordable prices for the foreseeable future. Otherwise they wouldn't have decided to move forward with it right?

USAOGM - What other incentives the region offer companies interested in re-locating here?

CAD - We do not have time to discuss all of the incentives available in detail but the Commonwealth of Pennsylvania offers competitive incentive packages relating to tax abatements, job creation tax credits, job training programs, low-interest business financing, ethane tax credits, among other things. Companies interested in establishing locations in Pennsylvania work directly with the Governor's Office through the Governor's Action Team GAT to coordinate an incentives & financing package. Additionally, GAT works with the company and any other relevant state departments to ensure efficient communication as well as acquisition of any necessary permits in an expeditious manner.

Additionally, the Commonwealth of Pennsylvania has an Office of International Business Development OIBD with representatives stationed in countries around the globe. OIBD provides guidance to foreign companies interested in investing in Pennsylvania on a variety of topics including legal & corporate structuring, taxes, workforce development, logistics & business partner identification.

USAOGM - Your final word if you have any- to say about this initiative?

CAD - We are just over a decade since the first well was drilled in the Marcellus Shale in 2004 by Range Resources and the Marcellus has already been a game-changer in terms of capital investment, job creation, and most notably, sheer energy production in the form of natural gas. I look forward to assisting energy-intensive companies take advantage of this historic opportunity by locating to the CORE PA region and utilizing our low-cost energy to meet their manufacturing needs.

USA Oil and Gas Monitor
For Daily News Report and Analysis • www.usaoilandgasmonitor.com

Bill Polacek CEO, President, and owner JWF Success Reveals- the True American Dream

Community Development

JWF has been incredibly essential to Pennsylvania as well. It has given back to the community that has helped it grow. JWF's entrepreneurship helped revive old buildings and provide employment to a lot of steel workers. The company, east located in rural Pennsylvania, has changed how the industry looks at manufacturing products.

The company also encourages young people to join them. A graduate from the local community college can work for JWF and the company pays his tuition in return. The company prizes good welders and provides training at its welding and training center- JWF Weld School. Apart from this, there are also two scholarships that encourage such talent.

JWF the Largest Manufacturing Plant in the East serves the Oil and Gas Industry among Other Industries in CORE PA

JWFI/ETC combines:
- Continuous technical training through JWF Weld School;
- Tuition reimbursement program- max $5250 per year, max under IRS rules, for those seeking continuing education or professional credentials;
- Career Pathing Initiative - emphasis on internal recruitment, other technical and professional development efforts through WedNet and other funding;
- Payment of student loans for those selected & who maintain employment with JWFI;
- John J. Polacek, Sr. Scholarship Program;
- Machining apprenticeship in March, 2014 at JWF Machining.

In a one on one interview with USAOGM Editor- Gloria Towolawi, Bill Polacek CEO JWF talks about the role his company is playing in CORE PA

Back in 1957, JWF Industries began because of the passion and drive of one man – John Polacek Sr. John was a steelworker with a family of nine children. He could barely make ends meet. He decided to go out on his own – so he mounted a welding machine on the back of his truck and Johnny's Welding was open for business. The first shop operated out of a small two room garage.

But the entrepreneurial spirit did not die out in one generation. John's son, Bill, worked for him when he was in school. He was ready to do this for lifetime, when John died. With a kid on the way, Bill made a strategic decision about this future – he bought his father's equipment from his mother for around ten to fifteen thousand dollars, and there he began his own dream.

What was a two room garage soon grew to become over a million square feet, and 2 employees to over 400 at present. Bill was featured on the front cover of the Forbes in 2004 – "Entrepreneur of the Year". He has also been recognized by the Governor for his entrepreneurship and job creation.

Manufacturing industries - JWF Industries Family of Companies

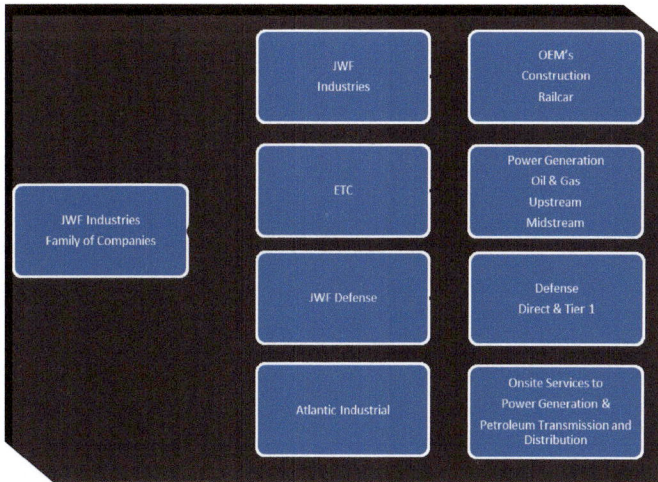

USA Oil and Gas Monitor
For Daily News Report and Analysis • www.usaoilandgasmonitor.com

JWF is primarily involved in the following industries and has the largest manufacturing plants.

- **Commercial and defense manufacturing** – The Company has been serving Tier 1 defense contractors since 2004. It has also armored 325 Humvees used in war. JWF aims to directly deal with the government as the next step in their growth.
- **Gas / Oil/ PowerGen Manufacturing Facility** – JWF had the insight to bank into the needs of the oil and gas industry right when it was beginning to flourish, back in 2011. The company was located strategically and found out the needs of the corporations around them and started serving them, thus saving them the cost of getting equipment from the southwest.
- **Vehicle Integration Centre** – Vehicle integration is done in a facility in Windber. The location provides enormous advantage, because the products built are huge, as much as eighty thousand gallons, and shipping them from here becomes easier.
- **ASME Large Tank Facility** – The Company has ASME American Society of Mechanical Engineering certification which means they can build pressure vehicles. The company manufactures API tanks, and condensers, etc.

The company has consistently manufactured equipment suited to the needs of its customers. WHY JWF- A One Call Solution

- Safe and Customer-Focused Approach
- Excellent longstanding reputation for customer satisfaction
- Quality
- Delivery
- Price
- Engineering and Design capabilities
- True "Turn Key" solution
- Located within close proximity to Marcellus/ Utica activity
- Lower transportation cost
- Reduced opportunity for transportation permitting issues
- Large facilities capable of handling projects, large and small

Bill see Shell Cracker plant coming to Beaver County in western Pennsylvania impacting his company in a positive way- bringing in more businesses.

USA Oil and Gas Monitor Subscription and Advert Rates

12 month Digital Subscription @ $119.88
12 month Print Subscription @ $144
Excludes taxes and shipping where applicable

New! *Our Digital and Print Editions is distributed by Amazon and Create Space; Globally and Nationwide to Energy and Petroleum Subscribers.*

Digital Edition Advert Rates
Full Page Advert $500
Half Page Advert $250

Print Edition Advert Rates
Full Page Advert $1000
Half Page Advert $650
Quarter Page Advert $350

For Online Advert Placement
Go online @
www.usaoilandgasmonitor.com/advertise

Request more info by emailing us today or go to **www.usaoilandgasmonitor.com/subscribe**

Jason Ritchey-president and CEO, Curry Supply

Curry Supply Products support both Drilling and Fracking Operations in the Oil and Gas Industry

At curry supply facility – equipment manufacturing and distribution capabilities was witnessed first-hand. Curry Supply management has this to say about its services and the turnkey solutions of its products to the industries they serve. See Except below.

USAOGM- Tell about yourself and what you do at Curry Supply?

Curry- Jason Ritchey, I am the Owner and President of Curry Supply Company. I am responsible for the growth, profitability, and sustainability of the company. All departments of the company report to me, including Sales, Marketing, Engineering, Manufacturing, Quality Control, Warranty, Parts, Service, and Shipping. I meet frequently with the managers from each of these departments to ensure that we are producing the highest quality products in the most efficient manner for our customers. National and international business development is important for the growth of our business, so I spend a great deal of time looking for emerging markets, analyzing trends, and finding opportunities to expand our product offerings. Our company has grown over the years by being flexible, responsive, and forward-looking. I intend to continue that tradition.

USAOGM - Give us a brief history of Curry Supply and Your products line?

Curry - Curry Supply is a family owned business that was established in 1932. At that time it was primarily an agricultural feed supplier. Over the past 84 years, Curry Supply has grown to be one of America's largest manufacturers and dealers of commercial service vehicles including on- and off-road water trucks, mechanics trucks, on- and off-road fuel/lube trucks, vacuum trucks, winch trucks, dump trucks, crash attenuator trucks, lube trailers, and lube skids. These products are used in the Construction, Mining, Oil & Gas, Waste, Equipment Rental, and Rail industries to service equipment used on the job sites.

Industries Served- Construction, Rental, Mining, Oil and Gas, Agriculture, waste and rail

USAOGM - What make your Products different from the competition? What is your company USP?

Curry - Curry Supply has built its reputation on several things that differentiate us from the competition. First, over our history, we have been willing - and able - to customize products quickly and efficiently. Second, we take extraordinary precautions to ensure that our products are of the highest quality possible. Our manufacturing facilities are ISO9001 certified, our Director of Quality inspects each product at every stage of the manufacturing process, and we test every product before shipment. Thirdly, unlike many competitors, Curry Supply provides a complete range of in-house services including engineering, tank manufacturing, fabrication, assembly, painting, testing, financing, warranty, parts/service, and delivery/shipping. Most competitors do not provide that many in-house services with the sale of their trucks. At Curry Supply, we pride ourselves on making the whole purchasing process easy for our customers.

USAOGM - Given the economic downturn in the oil and gas industry, how has this affected your production and how have you been able to weather the storm.

Curry - Fortunately for Curry Supply, we have a very diverse product line. Many of our commercial service vehicles are used across several different industries. If one industry is experiencing a downturn, others are not. As a result, our production is not affected very much. In addition, because of our willingness and capability of customizing products we have become

USA Oil and Gas Monitor
For Daily News Report and Analysis • www.usaoilandgasmonitor.com

a source for customers looking for solutions to unique applications. Also, over our history, we have been very aware of emerging markets and needs which has allowed us to create and introduce product lines for those markets. These factors have allowed Curry Supply to grow over the years regardless of how one particular market may fluctuate.

USAOGM - Pennsylvania is the second largest natural gas producer in the USA, what role your products plays in the oil and gas industry.

Curry - Curry Supply products provide operational support for both drilling and fracking operations. We also provide service support for the equipment used on the job site.

Capabilities
Full engineering staff for design and quality assurance

- State of the art tank fabrication systems
- Sand and shot blast capabilities
- Final assembly facilities
- Final inspection and test bays to ensure every piece of equipment is inspected and tested before delivery

Jeff Shaw-Sales Manager, Curry Supply

USA Oil and Gas Monitor
For Daily News Report and Analysis • www.usaoilandgasmonitor.com

SUBSCRIPTION FORM

First Name _____ Middle _____ Last _____

Current Job Title _____ Job Title Code _____

Company Name _____

Preferred Mailing Address - (Circle One)

    Business   Residence

Street _____ (No PO Boxes Please)

City _____ State _____ Zip _____

Country _____

Day Phone _____ If outside U.S., include country code. (ex: 000-000-000-0000)

Fax _____ Email _____

Form Instructions:
Email completed form to subscribe@usaoilandgasmonitor.com or mail form with check to the address below.

RGT Media Communications Corp.
10777 Westheimer Road #1100
Houston Texas 77042

1 Year Digital Subscription
For non-Texas subscribers - $119.88
Subscribers living in Texas – pays $119.88 plus 8.25% state tax $9.89 = $129.77

1 Year Print Subscription
For non-Texas subscribers - $144
Please add shipping cost and multiply by 12 (for example $1.67 x12) = 20.04
Subscribers living in Texas – pays $144 plus 8.25% state tax $11.88= $155.88
Please add shipping cost and multiply by 12 (for example $1.67 x12) = 20.04

Shipping Cost (calculated by weight)
Circle choice from the following option and add to the subscription cost

First Class 1- 5 business/days = $1.67

Fedex Shipping 1-3 business/days= $6.40

USPS Priority 1-3 business/days= $3.56

International First Class 1-7 business/days= $12.44

You can also pay for subscription online by visiting our website:
www.usaoilandgasmonitor.com/subscribe
Wire transfer, call Jewel Spring, 832-486-0095 for any questions.

Payment Method

Card Type (circle one)

Amex   Visa   Master   Discovery

Card No.

_____

Expiration Date

_____

CSV No.

_____

Name on Card

_____

By Check

Check No.

_____

USA Oil and Gas Monitor
For Daily News Report and Analysis • www.usaoilandgasmonitor.com

July 2016 • Issue 7

COREPAGLOBAL.COM

An International Media Tour of the

Manufacturing, Oil and Gas Facilities in CORE PA

USA Oil and Gas Monitor
For Daily News Report and Analysis • www.usaoilandgasmonitor.com

Noelle A. Long Project Manager & Regional Representative CORE PA Global speaks at the opening lunch of the Tour

CORE PA poised to Attract International Trade and FDI to the Oil and Gas, Mining Industries in Rural Pennsylvania

In a bid to attract more foreign direct investment and increase international trade CORE PA organized a media tour that includes international journalists from the following countries London, Australia, India, Canada, Nigeria and the USA. USA Oil and Gas Monitor represented the USA Media at this media Tour. An in-depth report of the Oil and Gas Industry, Construction and Mining Industry in Pennsylvania is reported By the Editor – Gloria Towolawi- USA Oil and Gas Monitor- Read the Media Tour Reports in this edition.

In a one on one interview- Noelle A. Long Project Manager & Regional Representative CORE PA Global speaks on this initiative:

USAOGM- Tell Us About Yourself?

CORE PA: I have been with SEDA Council of Government located in central Pennsylvania

COREPAGLOBAL.COM

for 13 years now. We are a local economic development agency working on a variety of different projects for both local governments, residents in the community, also different community organizations, and businesses. We have been providing trade assistance. Helping companies export their products and services for close to 30 years now. Just recently, we have gotten more into the foreign direct investment assistance services which is where CORE PA was born out of. I have been managing that project for almost three years. And also working on the trade side of things, helping companies export their products and services.

USAOGM- CORE PA vision, mission, and goals?

COREPA: We are tasked to promote a 53-county region of Pennsylvania, so that the more rural parts of Pennsylvania becomes an ideal location for companies to come establish manufacturing, establish sales headquarters, Research and Development facilities, etc. We are tasked with telling the story of the rest of Pennsylvania because often times, people just associate Pittsburgh and Philadelphia as the whole state, but there is more of a story to tell to promote the more rural regions of the state. We are doing this through promotion like the media familiarization tour we are doing right now. We have done Agriculture industry media tour and plastics industry media tour and the current one we are doing is focused on the oil and gas, mining and construction industries. We also attend international trade shows as well.

We are working with well over 50 economic development partners across the state. We are trying to do a more coordinated approach to promoting the rest of the state. Some of these more rural economic development professionals, might not have the resources or the capabilities to promote their smaller county but when we combine our forces together, we are a bit more of a stronger voice and we are able to get a bit more exposure for those lesser known regions of Pennsylvania.

We are hoping that by first September that we can have our first announcement that correlate to our efforts as CORE PA. That's pretty exciting.

COREPA- Access to market:

- Strategic location within 40 per cent of the US market and more than 60 per cent of Canada's market is located within an 800 km radius of the CORE region
- 3 major sea ports - including the Port of Philadelphia which provides access to more major cities than by rail and truck
- 6 international airports
- Over 138,000 km of streams and rivers, 9 trillion liters of surface water, 300 trillion liters of groundwater
- Pennsylvania ranks 5th in the United States for rail infrastructure boasting over 8,000 km of track and 66 operating railroads
- An established and diverse supply chain that is ready to meet your specific needs

- Home to more than 2,100 foreign owned companies

Oil and Gas Industry

Pennsylvania is the 2nd largest producer of natural gas in the United States. 25,000 natural gas wells drilled in Pennsylvania since 2007. Pennsylvania boasts both Utica and Marcellus Shale plays. Shale gas is driving down energy costs. Wholesale electricity prices have declined 40 per cent since 2007.

If the Marcellus Shale Region was a country its gas production would rank 3rd in the world behind the United States and Russia.

Pennsylvania broke the record by producing 4 trillion cubic feet of cleaning-burning energy in 2014.

Three $1 billion USD natural gas power plants coming on-line starting in 2016.

Pennsylvania named 2014 FDI Destination of the Future for Energy Intensive Industries. Pennsylvania has shown positive FDI growth since 2012.

FDI contributes to 70,000 jobs in CORE PA, ranking Pennsylvania 4th in the United States in job creation.

CORE PA contributes to the 8th largest manufacturing output in the United States.

Construction and Mining Industry

- The CORE region is home to more than 900 construction related companies employing more than 7,600 workers.

USA Oil and Gas Monitor
For Daily News Report and Analysis • www.usaoilandgasmonitor.com

Intl Journalists and Editor USAOGM in the Extreme Right -side -Meet the Media Team

- Pennsylvania's 12-year transportation plan calls for $63.2 billion USD for roads, bridges, railroads and transit with other prominent end-user industries including oil & gas, mining and manufacturing.
- Advances in horizontal drilling and hydraulic fracking have made oil and gas accessible and have made an impact on construction equipment sectors.
- Pennsylvania is the 2nd largest producer of natural gas in the United States.
- Pennsylvania is the 4th largest coal producer in the United States and is the only state producing anthracite.
- The global construction & mining machinery market is expected to grow at an annual rate of 9.3 per cent through 2018 making Pennsylvania a prime location for suppliers.
- The region has more than 50 mining industry supply companies.

Economic and Employment diversification
Manufacturing in Pennsylvania

- The manufacturing industry is the foundation of Pennsylvania's economy — which means we have the skills, experience, and knowledge to help companies succeed in the United States
- Throughout the history of our nation, Pennsylvania has been a leader in manufacturing, and you will find that our world-class R&D institutions, technology commercialization programs, technical and industrial resources, and skilled workforce combine to create a unique advantage for businesses
- Manufacturing Industry Impact in Pennsylvania
- $82 billion in economic impact. Source: bea.gov, GDP By State 2015Q3
- 8th largest manufacturing output in the United States. Source: bea.gov, GDP By State 2015Q3
- 14,520+ manufacturing establishments. Source: PA Dept. of Labor & Industry, 2015Q4
- 19,770 employers. Source: PA Dept. of Labor & Industry, 2015Q4
- 563,600 employees. Source: PA Dept. of Labor & Industry, 2015Q4
- $63,752 average annual wage. Source: PA Dept. of Labor & Industry, 2015Q4
- Top manufacturing industries (by employment) Source: PA Dept. of Labor & Industry, 2015Q4
  - Fabricated Metal Products – 82,485
  - Food – 69,637
  - Machinery – 47,669
  - Chemicals – 40,243
  - Transportation Equipment – 39,726
  - Primary Metals – 38,363
  - Plastics & Rubber Products – 36,839
  - Computer & Electronic Products – 30,997

Foreign Direct investment FDI incentives
COREPA -The Keystone Opportunities Zone is a state-wide program that designated land and buildings to companies for up to 10 years - with zero taxes paid to the state. This is the primary incentive but then there are also some more local incentives based on the economic development partner, who on their own can give incentives for example- they are able to say, "Well on top of the Keystone Opportunity Zone, we are also giving

you this incentive to locate in our business park," etc.

We also have some industry specific funding for things like research and development, tax credits as well. Those are, depending on what industry sector you are looking at and certainly the business resources that are available. For example, free assistance- All my services are free to companies to help them expand their global footprint. We have a network of 15 authorized trade representatives around the world that are basically at the beck and call of Pennsylvania companies to find new distributors, to find new customers to help wade through different regulations with different countries.

Workforce Training Incentives
- Training programs offering up to 50 per cent savings on new hire training costs
- Tax incentive programs
- Industry partnerships savings on group training

Talent and Education
- More than 100 educational institutions offering customized training programs to industry
- Legacy workforce prepared for various industries

Noelle A. Long

CORE PA Funding Source?
COREPA- We were a recipient of federally awarded Make It In America challenge grant 3 years ago. That is supported by the federal government, actually 3 different federal arms because we have 3 different moving parts to this CORE PA initiative. We have the promotion side of things, which is what we are doing on a daily basis, the trade shows, the media tours but there

Media Tour Journalist introductory breakfast with COREPA Team

is also a workforce component that looks at training needs of companies looking to expand and also come into the region.

And finally we have the industrial resource centers that have focused their efforts on studying the total cost of ownership for current Pennsylvania companies as well as supply chain analysis. There are key industries that we can look at for already established companies to begin looking at reshoring their products. Also because it is such a strong opportunity, we can target those industries from an FDI perspective.

In Summary
CORE PA Global is an initiative established to increase the visibility of a 53-county footprint of Pennsylvania, USA to international and domestic investors. CORE PA partners with over 50 economic development organizations and the Commonwealth of Pennsylvania to attract, retain, and grow business and industry in our region.

FOR OVER 20 YEARS WE HAVE BEEN FACILITATING FOREIGN DIRECT INVESTMENT AND INTERNATIONAL TRADE

Pennsylvania is a leader in international business development efforts. The state boasts nearly 20 professionals dedicated to trade and investment promotion in the capital, 10 Regional Export Network REN offices, 19 Authorized Trade Representatives, and 12 Authorized Investment Representatives strategically located around the globe. In the last five years, this local, on-the-ground assistance has resulted in over 40,000 jobs, over $3B in documented export sales, over $575M in capital investment!

Carbon Steel/ high yield pipe fittings

Ezeflow Group the Largest Manufacturer of Pipe Fitting in North America

With a longstanding reputation for delivering only the highest quality products all over the world, Ezeflow Group is the largest and most diverse manufacturer of pipe fittings in North America. For over 40 years, Ezeflow has been manufacturing a large selection of materials in all sizes, for every possible shape and configuration.

Since the company first opened its doors in 1972, Ezeflow has worked diligently to stay well ahead of the competition. Today, they offer products in an array of metal specialties, including corrosion resistant alloys, clad metals, and carbon + chrome-molybdenum. In additions, fittings can be made in an assortment of sizes, starting with just a 1/2" and going through 60", which is a size range that most manufacturers are unable to accommodate.

CAPABILITIES

FROM PLATE:
4 inch to 84 inch 100 mm to 2140 mm outside diameters.

FROM WELDED TUBULAR PRODUCTS:
½ inch to 84 inch 12 mm to 2140 mm outside diameters, up to schedule 160 and more.

FROM SEAMLESS TUBULAR PRODUCTS:
½ inch to 36 inch 12 mm to 900 mm outside diameters, up to schedule 160 and more.

WALL THICKNESS up to 4 inch 100 mm. EVERY SHAPE AND CONFIGURATION

Ezeflow is able to manufacture fittings that are designed to meet a client's specific needs. Ezeflow pipe fittings are made for everything from mining and offshore oil drilling platforms to desalinization plants and power generation for coal, natural gas, and nuclear. The company prides itself on 24/7 manufacturing and delivery, including same-day and overnight delivery.

Why Relocate to Pennsylvania

Although Ezeflow's headquarters are located in Canada, the company previously had a warehouse in Houston, Texas. Due to a downturn in the market, as well as a need to cut overhead costs, the warehouse was relocated to New Castle, PA after purchasing Flowline Corp. in 2011. The move to PA, which is the second largest natural gas producer in the US, also allows those in the Marcellus Shale and Utica Shale drilling industry easy access to any fittings they may need, especially in situations that require urgent maintenance. Most importantly, the state and local government – Lawrence County in Pennsylvania helped Ezeflow to secure a $6 million loan – low interest for the company to retool its plant. The state has also helped with export grants.

The residents of New Castle and the surrounding areas have also benefited from the warehouse's relocation. About 90 new technician jobs have been created.

Currently, Shell is moving forward with plans to build a multi-billion dollar ethane cracker plant along the banks of the Ohio River in Township, in western Pennsylvania -Beaver County. In a recent press release, Shell reported they expected the project to be complete by 2020 or 2021 and planned to use shale gas producers in the Utica and Marcellus basins to produce over 1 million tons of polyurethane every year. Ezeflow fully expects to see an increase in sales when the Shell plant starts.

Shell Cracker Plant Coming to Pennsylvania- Stakeholders and Communities React

Following the statement by Governor Wolf that he was notified by Shell that they would build their ethane cracker plant in Pennsylvania: According to the release-

"Over the past four years, the Commonwealth of Pennsylvania has worked with Royal Dutch Shell to finalize plans to construct an ethane cracker plant in Western Pennsylvania, and this morning I was notified that Shell has taken the final step to move ahead with this game-changing plant and create thousands of jobs in Pennsylvania.

"The commonwealth began its efforts on this project in 2012, and I would like to thank former Governor Tom Corbett and his Secretary of Community and Economic Development C. Alan Walker for all of their efforts to bring the plant to Western Pennsylvania.

"Since first taking office, I have worked in close collaboration with my Secretary of Community and Economic Development Dennis Davin, the Pittsburgh Regional Alliance, local officials in Western Pennsylvania, and Royal Dutch Shell to make the proposed plant a reality. The commonwealth engaged the company with the goal of creating jobs, spurring economic development, and taking the next steps to connect the energy industry with long-term, sustainable economic growth.

"My administration is committed to creating jobs in the energy industry through responsible, well-regulated extraction and long-term, creative industrial growth. We have worked to develop strategies for safe and responsible pipeline development that brings resources to markets and facilities and we have prioritized the Shell plant to show the world that Pennsylvania is a leader in energy manufacturing and downstream production.

"The success of this project is part of a much-needed, longer term plan to translate our abundant resources to make Pennsylvania a leader in downstream production. The commitment of the Shell cracker plant in Western Pennsylvania is an important step toward this goal.

"This critical effort spanned four years, and two administrations, and today I want to congratulate all of those involved, including both Republican and Democratic officials, and thank Royal Dutch Shell for providing this unique and exciting economic development opportunity to the people of Western Pennsylvania."

Stakeholders' Reactions

Ezeflow Group Vice President Mr. Marty Capoferri says, "There will be a lot of business. There's a lot of other subcontracting work; it will be a big benefit for us.

JWF Industries CEO- Bill Polacek says- "It will impact us in a lot of ways. It's going to create a need for a lot more storage of their product, and a lot of high-pressure vessels. While they are building the plant, they are going to need a lot of what we are manufacturing here for the oil and gas industry".

Paul A. McCloskey, VP of Energy and Business Development Clearfield County says, "I am excited about what it means for the rest of Pennsylvania's economy! The Shell cracker plant will be located in Beaver County, PA which is actually just outside of the CORE PA region. Regardless though, it's a fantastic announcement and this decision will essentially create an entirely new industry in western-PA".

Jeff Kotula, President Washington County Chamber of Commerce says, "It will be very good for us because it will shows our reputation as energy producer in the United States. By having the cracker plant, demonstrates that an international company, has seen and put their stamp of approval on what we doing in Pennsylvania and in the tri-counties. More importantly, we have to take that energy, build the necessary infrastructure, and get it to market not only for residential usage but also for commercial and industrial use. That will benefit us on a long term in ensuring that our natural gas resolution continues not only for Pennsylvania but also continue our country's energy independence".

About the Shell Project

This project is the result of more than four years of planning over the course of two administrations

Project Facts

- This week's announcement that Shell Chemical will proceed with building a cracker plant in Southwestern Pennsylvania is a game-changer - both for the region and the commonwealth as a whole.
- This announcement marks the first major U.S. project of its type outside the Gulf Coast Region, with projections of employment of up to 6,000 during peak construction periods and a commitment of 600 full-time positions in the future.
- A key factor in securing this project was the many years of consistent and well-coordinated statewide collaboration. Over the past four years, the Commonwealth of Pennsylvania worked with Shell to finalize plans to construct this facility. Beginning in 2012 with the last administration, this project was seamlessly transitioned to the Wolf Administration. Since first taking office, Governor Wolf has worked in close collaboration with the Secretary of Community and Economic Development Dennis Davin and the Governor's Action Team, the Pittsburgh Regional Alliance, local officials in Southwestern Pennsylvania to propel this project across the finish line.
- The action is not only profound as it relates to an estimated economic impact of $6 billion or the thousands of jobs that accompany a project of this magnitude, but it is also profound when placed in context of what this means for all of Pennsylvania's industry sectors.
- The new cracker plant in Beaver County will make plastics from gas extracted in Pennsylvania and help attract industries that use these natural gas byproducts for the goods they produce.
- This means that the facility will serve as the centerpiece in the region for the creation of new markets for polyethylene with added potential of attracting additional manufacturing investments that will lead to even more business attraction and job creation for generations to come.
- Located on the site of the former Horsehead zinc smelter in Potter and Center townships in Beaver County, Southwestern Pennsylvania.
- As with any project of this magnitude, we have to ensure we are protecting the health of our environment and our people, and Shell has demonstrated a commitment to effective and responsible development of the site with a focus on protecting the environment and working together with residents and the local community to chart a path forward.
- The commonwealth has also conducted an exhaustive review of Shell's proposals, and after several public hearings, granted permits that we are confident will protect the air, water and soil in the area.
- Governor Wolf is committed to creating jobs through responsible, well-regulated natural gas extraction and long-term, creative industrial growth.
- We have worked to develop strategies for safe and responsible pipeline development that brings resources to markets and facilities.

CAB World Class Cable Rings and Saddles manufactured by the blind and handicap in CORE PA

CAB Products Support Power and Control Cables under Pipeline Structure, Refineries etc.

Allen Smith- General Manager, CAB

In a continuation of the media Tour of manufacturing, oil and gas facilities in CORE PA- I got to learn about a very unique and humanitarian organization named Cambria County Association for the Blind & Handicapped-CAB- a Company that has cable management system solutions for all industries – including the oil and gas industry. What is unique about their products is the people that manufactures the products- the blind and Handicapped.

Allen Smith- General Manager in an interview with Gloria Towolawi – Editor USAOGM explains.

USAOGM -Tell us about yourself and what you do at CAB?

CAB - I am the Ebensburg Division General Manager. I have been with CAB for 41 years and am in charge of overall operations.

USAOGM -Give us a brief history of CAB and Your products line?

CAB - Cambria County Association for the Blind and Handicapped-CAB is a private, non-profit organization dedicated to providing job opportunities and services to persons with disabilities. CAB Products are manufactured by CAB employees with great pride and integrity.

> We manufacture an amazing variety of products, and we sell them all over the world.

From mops and rugs to cable hangers, hooks, and reflective safety garments, through the years the Cambria County Association for the Blind and Handicapped has manufactured a wide range of useful items. Some of which are:

CAB stainless steel cable rings and saddles

Consistent high quality makes CAB Products ideal for extreme conditions in both above and below ground applications. Along the Artic Ocean on the North Slope of Alaska, CAB stainless steel cable rings and saddles provide safe, strong support for electrical cables that run under oil pipelines. CAB specializes in hangers for these types of high corrosive environments.

CAB Cable Rings and Saddles offer the highest quality support for all types of solar panel wiring. The product have plenty of capacity for large bundles of string wiring. For over 35 years, electrical engineers have specified CAB Products in the most corrosive and demanding environments around the world.

Heavy Duty Hangers and J-Hooks

Safe, strong support for electrical cables, hoses and pipes. CAB's standard J-Hooks are made from .180" x 1" 4.6 x 25.4mm safety edge steel. For added safety and protection, they have a heavy 80 mil 2mm coating of high-visibility orange plastisol.

CAB's high dielectric grade plastisol has a 400 volt per mil dielectric breakdown strength and is flame retardant. It is tough, durable and extremely resistant to corrosion. Available in sizes up to 12" 305mm diameter in a wide variety of configurations.

USAOGM -What make your Products different from the competition? What is unique about your product?

USA Oil and Gas Monitor
For Daily News Report and Analysis • www.usaoilandgasmonitor.com

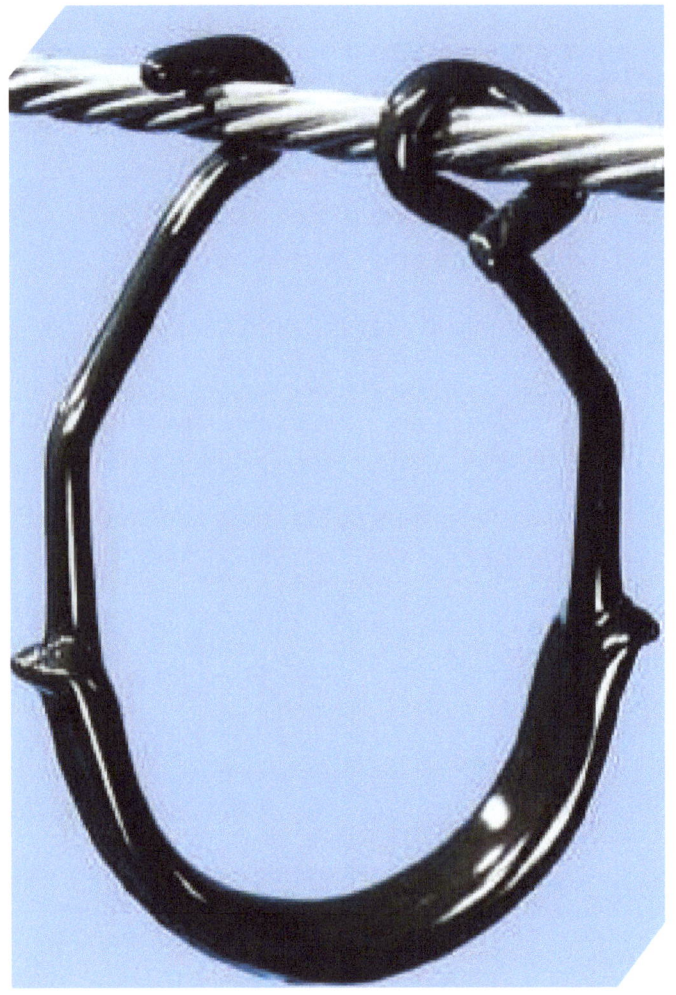

100 percent PVC Coated Type 316 Stainless Steel or Galvanized Steel

CAB - CAB manufactures its product line of cable rings and saddles from high tensile strength spring steel for maximum strength and durability. Many of the products are 100 per cent PVC coated for excellent durability in highly corrosive environments. The coating also provides added safety and protection for all types of data, control, electrical and communication cables. The CAB coatings are flame retardant, high dielectric grade, UV stabilized and extremely resistant to corrosion. All cutting, forming, coating and other manufacturing operations are conducted in CAB's, modern, state-of-the-art 84,000 square foot facility. CAB's mission is to provide employment opportunities for persons with disabilities while producing high quality products for our customers worldwide.

USAOGM - Given the fact that your product is produced by the Blind and Handicapped individuals, how does this help position the services you offer as well as your products.

CAB - Our customers have been very supportive of our efforts to provide employment to persons with disabilities and also providing high quality support services.

USAOGM - What percentage of your special needs workforce produces this cable hangers?

CAB - All CAB hangers are manufactured by employees with disabilities. We have approximately 400 employees.

USAOGM - What is the criteria to hire these special need individuals - in your organization?

CAB - Nearly 300 individuals with disabilities work at the Cambria County Association for the Blind and Handicapped. Having a regular job, earning a paycheck, and doing something productive gives our unique workforce independence and confidence. It makes their lives better in many ways.

Vocational Rehabilitation
Having a disability does not mean you cannot work. Through vocational rehabilitation we teach people how to work despite their disability.

It begins with vocational aptitude testing, in which our rehabilitation staff evaluates each individual's capabilities, strengths, and interests. Then using those results, we provide one on one professional training in skill areas such as packaging, assembly, metals-forming, industrial sewing, welding, cleaning, and material-handling. The training is highly individualized and usually leads to long term employment at CCABH or elsewhere in the community.

CAB products cables and hangers on display

Personal Work Adjustment Training

Personal Work Adjustment Training is provided to help our disabled employees learn appropriate behavior and problem solving both on the job and in daily living. They receive practical training in things like budgeting, banking, and comparative shopping. While in this program, individuals have opportunities to experience a sampling of production jobs.

School-To-Work

Our School-To-Work program is offered to high school students with disabilities. It provides a professional assessment of their capabilities and employment training while still in school.

On-The-Job Training

It is our goal to place each employee with a disability in his or her appropriate level of work. Our staff provides on-the-job training and job-coaching services to local employers who offer opportunities for qualified workers with disabilities

USAOGM -Pennsylvania is the second largest natural gas producer in the USA, what role does your products plays in the oil and gas industry.

CAB- Our products are primarily used for the support of power and control cables under pipeline structure. The oil pipeline in Alaska uses CAB Cable Rings and Saddles for the support of all power and control cables used in developing new oil wells that feed the main Alaska Pipeline. They are used extensively downstream for running power, control and communication cables in refineries, chemical plants and other types of mills and plants.

Advertise With Us

USA Oil and Gas Domain Analysis- For Online Advert Placement
Google Page Rank 4: An authority site for oil, gas and energy news
Global Rank Worldwide: 14,838,812
Estimated Monthly Visit: 2.5 million
Search: 94.68%
Source: Checkpagerank.net

New! Our Digital Edition is distributed by Amazon Kindle Select- Guarantees 1 billion Audience Reach on Amazon.

Print Edition

Distributed by Create Space- An Amazon company; globally and nationwide. Available on CreateSpace Direct, Major Bookstores and Online Retailers, Libraries and Academic Institutions, Amazon.com, Amazon Europe, Amazon UK
Search for your monthly copy on Amazon with our ISBN: 1533437358- First week of every month!
Download media kit: http://usaoilandgasmonitor.com/advertise
Call Advert Hotline: 832-486-0095

USA Oil and Gas Monitor
For Daily News Report and Analysis • www.usaoilandgasmonitor.com

Robert H. Beatty, Jr.- CEO O" Ring gives his presentation

Oring Sunnyside Energy Park Project shows CNG/LNG as a Viable Alternative Fuel

Clean energy sources are one of the major issues in the twenty first century. With concerns for the environment on the rise and the hunt for sustainable sources of energy gaining importance, CNG is clearly emerging as the fuel of the future. The environment cannot sustain fossil fuels in the longer term. Diesel, for instance, is known to be carcinogenic.

The benefits that CNG can provide are not just academic or ideal – they have proven themselves in the real world. A small country like Pakistan has three million cars running on natural gas, so it is definitely a viable alternative.

O" Ring CNG Fuel Systems, L.P

Oring started the business of producing CNG for cars back in 2010. It began from a realization of how central an energy source is to the earth and its problems – and how it is a common issue for everyone irrespective of their political or ideological leanings. Oring is now looking to develop a project that will prove the positives of the natural gas approach.

"O" Ring CNG is a PA-based company dedicated to both promoting and providing the pathway for the use of CNG as a vehicle fuel with over 30 years' experience in the natural gas and compression industry. "O" Ring CNG is certified by the Natural Gas Vehicle Institute NGVI of America in both CNG Fuel Station Design & Construction and CNG Fuel Station Management.

The Project -
SUNNYSIDE ENERGY PARK, LLC

The project aims to build CNG and LNG production, distribution, and fueling stations in the Sunnyside Energy Park. The project is the first of its kind that envisions small scale production and dispensing of natural gas, as at present, natural gas is produced en masse and then transported via rail and trucking to the distribution centers.

The stations, however, are only part of a larger plan in which the benefits and sustainability of the entire alternative benefit project will be demonstrated. The end goal is a much larger alternative energy park and distribution Centre. Synthetic gasoline SYN-GAS, Methanol, Ethanol, Dimethyl Ether DME and Olefin production and a brine water/ produced water treatment facility are the second stage projects that will complete the alternative energy park as a whole.

Integrated power modules will also be installed. This will allow the site to manufacture its own electricity and heat, directly through natural gas.

The benefits to Local Economy and Environment

The new CNG and LNG stations will have an impact on energy resources by providing another option in vehicle fuel for local residents. It will also give more citizens and businesses the chance to utilize natural gas as a vehicle fuel and enjoy fuel savings will supporting the local economy. Since the primary fuel supply for this station is PA natural gas its' use will in turn lessen the demand for foreign oil and move the Commonwealth another step closer to energy independence. As the demand for oil decreases, the price should also stabilize, making it a less volatile energy source as Americans rely more heavily on our own energy sources.

Car running on CNG Fuel

CNG/LNG as a fuel not only provides environmental benefits, but also provides greater savings. At the end of the day, when something is being marketed to the end consumers, cost effectiveness makes the difference in whether this can be a sustainable change or not. Apart from increasing savings, the CNG industry also makes a difference by proving employment in the area, and all of these are differences people can feel and see for themselves.

Number of Spin-off Jobs, Construction Jobs, and Full Time Jobs according to CH4 USA, LLC

Construction jobs: CH4 USA, LLC projects that five 5 to six 6 temporary construction jobs will be created with this project to aid in site preparation and installation of equipment.

Spin-off jobs: According to the Marcellus Shale Coalition, between eight 8 and seventeen 17 full time jobs are created with each new alternative fuel station for maintenance, support, and parts/supply.

Estimated Environmental Benefits and Methodology

According the Environmental Protection Agency's online greenhouse gas equivalencies calculator http://www.epa.gov/cleanenergy/energy-resources/calculator.html, this project can reduce CO2 equivalent emissions by 71,760 metric tons per year, by year 4. That amount of reduced emissions is also equivalent to removing 15,107 passenger vehicles from the road each year, 25,720 tons of waste from landfills each year, 9,871 homes electricity use for one year, or 77,078,496 pounds of coal burned.

According to the US Department of Energy natural gas vehicles, whether CNG or LNG, also result in the following reductions in vehicular emissions, making both fuels a smarter choice to aid in the reduction of air pollution. Natural gas vehicles have shown to reduce vehicular emissions by the following amounts:

- 30 per cent in Greenhouse Gases GHG
- 30 per cent in Carbon Dioxide CO2
- 75 per cent Carbon Monoxide CO
- 55 per cent in Nitrogen Oxide NOx
- 95 per cent in Particulate Matter PM
- 55 per cent in Volatile Organic Compounds VOCs

With a secondary goal of this project being

Oring CNG Fuel Station

on-site electric generation, the site will be self-sustaining and independent of the public electrical power grid. Therefore there will be no need for metering, connection to the electric utility, etc. to sell/purchase electricity on a regular basis. The energy source for both electric and CNG/LNG generation is natural gas, supplied by on-site shallow wells through two independent suppliers. It is another economic benefit to the local economy.

Estimated Cost

The total estimated cost of this project is fourteen million five hundred, fifty-eight thousand, two hundred and fifty dollars $14,558,250, which includes the purchase of compressors, dryers, refrigeration and filtration units, CNG and LNG storage tanks, permitting costs, construction, site upgrades, and equipment installation.

Start and Completion Dates

Equipment will be ordered immediately and site preparation will begin during the summer months of 2016.

The estimated total completion time for the project is approximately 18 months, with a goal of completion by first quarter 2018.

The new CNG/LNG station will eventually be able to produce up to 50,000 GGE's of CNG/LNG per day, although the anticipated capacity will remain at 3,000 GGE's per day for the first year. At the one year mark post-expansion, the station projects distributing approximately 2000 additional GGE's per day with continued increasing demand to approximately 1500 additional GGE's per day by year two and continuing through years three and four. By year four it is projected that 1.4 m additional GGE's will be consumed annually.

In Summary

The benefits of converting to CNG or LNG for any fleet are tremendous, but for Pennsylvania residents in particular, these natural gas options hold even more opportunities. By utilizing a natural resource that is found within PA borders, CNG and LNG infrastructure growth has widespread trickle down effects on the local economy. Not only are consumers saving 30-50 per cent in fuel costs at the pump, but the sales of CNG and LNG will also result directly in an increased market for PA natural gas. Increased demand leads to increased drilling in the Marcellus Shale industry as well as a market for shallow gas well production, which will provide more jobs for Pennsylvanians and increased business for the multitude of vendors that support the drilling industry. The combined effect is increased disposable income for vendors and consumers alike that will benefit all aspects of the Pennsylvania economy.

Gloria Towolawi- Editor USAOGM and Robert H. Beatty, Jr.- CEO O Ring

About Robert H. Beatty, Jr. - CEO O" Ring CNG Fuel Systems, L.P

Mr. Beatty has 33 years' experience in the natural gas and compression industries with 17 years as the president of "O" Ring & Associates, Inc. as well as 9 years as CEO of "O" Ring CNG Fuel Systems, L.P., & Affiliated Entities which he founded in 2008. Mr. Beatty is also a professional educator, having taught at the university level for more than 25 years. He continues his educational outreach today through various seminars and speaking engagements where he demonstrates the benefits of CNG / Alternative Fuels/ and Energy Security. He holds certifications from the Natural Gas Vehicle Institute of America in both CNG Fuel Station Design & Construction and CNG Fuel Station Management. He has extensive experience with compressed gases as a technician, system designer, consultant, sales manager, and distributor for several major international compressor brands. From assessing the best plan for each customer, designing, building, and installing individualized equipment, to both routine and emergency service and maintenance, Mr. Beatty has the expertise and technical knowledge to diagnose and solve any compression, natural gas, or CNG challenge. He was awarded the 2013 Pittsburgh Business Times Energy Leadership Award for his efforts in revolutionizing the US transportation industry.

USA Oil and Gas Monitor
For Daily News Report and Analysis • www.usaoilandgasmonitor.com

Noise Solutions Incorporated provide Turnkey Solutions for the Energy and Mining Industries

Scott MacDonald President NSI lead the tour of his facility

Noise Solutions USA Incorporated NSI applies their trademark "science of silence" to provide engineered turnkey industrial noise control for oil and gas, mining, power and aerospace industries. Using its engineering and architectural expertise, the company develops high quality noise attenuation products. The inventory ranges from acoustic buildings, walls, enclosures and ventilation, to engine exhaust and cooler fan silencers.

Why Locate an Office in CORE PA
Headquartered in Alberta, Canada, the noise control company opened its second vertically integrated enterprise, United States East US East operations, in Sharon, Pennsylvania in 2014. The State Governor's Action Team and Penn-Northwest Development Corporation were instrumental in the NSI decision to locate its plant in CORE PA. Tax incentives were available due to NSI's substantial contribution to Mercer County, Pennsylvania's economy. One strong indication of a boost in prosperity is the return of a number of skilled workers who previously left the area to seek employment.

A portion of the financing was invested in job training for the over 200 new employment opportunities required for the plant's success. Additional funding was provided by other local organizations such as Shenango Valley Enterprise Zone and Sharon Industrial Development Authority. This community support was essential to NSI and its 55,000 square manufacturing plant and office space.

NSI Products
Occupational noise affects environmental health and safety. Studies and experience prove sustained exposure can lead to permanent hearing damage. To avoid this hazard it must be addressed during the early planning phase of renovations to current facilities or development of new businesses. NSI designs a Noise Suppression Blueprint that prioritizes the concerns of facility operators and regulators in conjunction with residential quality of life issues. This strategic noise plan optimizes area resources.

As a past recipient of the Oil and Gas Award, this leading North American supplier confidently promotes the most efficient equipment and reliable service. NSI's innovative product range meets both acoustic and operational requirements of industry clients. The Emcon Emissions Control Exhaust Silencer masters engine noise and $Co2$ outflow. Acoustically treated building ventilation sweeps cooling air across engines and compressors to maintain comfortable temperatures. Cooler fan silencers effectively attenuate noise of all frames, walls, outlets, and bottoms. Pipe lagging

The EmCon Emissions Control Exhaust Silencer

designs control intrusive sounds of waste water flow through pipes and fittings. Noise Solutions' self-framing buildings offer an economical alternative to conventional rigid-framed enclosures. NSI continues the research and design of excellent equipment at low cost ownership.

NCI proclaims new approaches to old problems in all facets of noise abatement at the most cost efficient prices. The plant in Sharon is one part of the company's overall global expansion goals. As the demand for its analysis, manufacturing, and design capabilities grows, it appears that the company will continue to increase its accessibility.